Create The Perfect Day

CREATE A LIFE YOU DESIRE

INCREASE PRODUCTIVITY

BE HAPPY

Jessica Peterson

Perfect Day Press

Create The Perfect Day / Jessica Peterson. -- 1st ed. / Perfect Day Press, an imprint of Manifest Publishing
ISBN 978-1-944913-30-4

Contents

Dedication

This book is dedicated to my husband Evan and daughter Cadence. They make my perfect day perfect.

Foreword

Written by Barry Habib

There's a big difference in getting through the day or getting from the day. While the vast majority of individuals do their best to make it through the day, one of the keys to success is gaining forward progress and momentum from each and every day.

It all starts with a plan.

Most individuals play defense each day by handling tasks that are thrown at them and doing their best to complete them. While this is admirable, it's very different than starting each day with a plan that keeps you on offense...that keeps you gaining ground...keeps you moving ahead towards your goals. To use a sports metaphor, you only score when you are on offense. Far too many people spend their day playing defense, instead of grabbing the ball and looking to score by having a plan to succeed each and every day.

It's great to see individuals have a one-year plan or a five-year plan, but the work has to get done each day. Strides must be made on a daily basis. It all starts when you *Create The Perfect Day*.

It has often been said that it's not what you know, it's who you know. Jessica Peterson is one of the best connectors that I've ever met. Jessica has mastered the art of helping her contacts gain more of the who you know connections.

I've never had a conversation with Jessica where she has not asked, "What can I do to help you?" or "Let me think of whom I can put you in touch with." Jessica has a sincere desire to help others succeed. One of the effective ways she does this is by making connections. It should also be noted that Jessica does not just ask these questions, she immediately follows up with putting people in touch with each other so that they can assist with growing their businesses.

Jessica has achieved high levels of success for herself, and I truly appreciate her motivation in reaching these levels. Jessica looks at the financial rewards and recognition as byproducts of her true motivation, which is to assist the growth and development of others. She uses her talents and personal experience to inspire and lead others towards achieving their personal goals.

We could all take a page out of Jessica's book in becoming better connectors and showing servant leadership. It's these types of individuals who become magnetic and draw others to them. Think about the people you are most drawn to. They are often the ones who have had a positive influence or who have made important connections for you. It's the people who you can learn from, as they guide you and help you move towards your own goals.

But it's not just about business when it comes to assisting others or making connections. Personal matters are often much more important. Many successful individuals have a hard time balancing work and their personal lives. Jessica, like so many of us, has gone through difficult personal times and crisis. These experiences have given Jessica both strength and empathy, which helps her guide others to find the confidence to persevere, as well as an understanding of what they could be going through. I have always admired Jessica's deep and sincere desire to want to assist others and bring out the best in them. The perfect day is not just about business.

About Barry Habib

Barry is an American Entrepreneur and frequent Media resource for his Mortgage and Housing expertise. He is the CEO of MBS Highway; a company and platform created to help mortgage professionals and Real Estate Agents articulate the opportunity in the housing market for their clients, along with a better understanding of the interest rate environment.

Barry is a well-known professional speaker on the financial and Real Estate markets and has had a long tenure with monthly appearances on CNBC and FOX. He was named the top Real Estate forecaster by Zillow and Pulsenomics and has been presented with the Crystal Ball Award for the most accurate Real Estate forecasts out of 150 of the top economists in the US.

Learn more about Barry from his website:

https://www.mbshighway.com/

A special message for you...

People say a perfect day seems unreal. When they ask me, what is a perfect day? I advise them that, "Every day is perfect because you are alive! Why not create a life you desire, increase productivity, and be happy?"

People's eyes light up after sharing this small but powerful statement. Every day we are alive is a true gift.

Now let's talk some more about what a perfect day means.

Time is one thing we can never get back. What we do with our beautiful gift of life is up to us, nobody else. Each of us have our strengths, loves, passions. We were given them for a reason. Dreams were given to us for a reason.

My friends and clients who are business professionals have shared with me that they have a dream, but can feel overwhelmed. They feel as if they are behind on making what they desire come true. They find their days come and go so fast with overwhelm.

A few of my real estate clients were overwhelmed in business. They did not know what the best plan was based on what they wanted to achieve. As we dove into what they really lights them up, we focused on creating their perfect days so they can LIVE with purpose and LOVE their days.

Create a life you desire.

Increase productivity.

Be happy.

Do you feel overwhelmed? Have lost clarity and/or focus?

Do you desire structure to have balance in your life, making the best use of your time and fulfill your dreams?

Good news! *Create The Perfect Day* is here to stop the overwhelm, gain clarity, be focused and productive.

So often I hear people say the first word that comes to mind when working with me is inspiration. This book is about inspiration, about how you can find your own inspiration to ignite your dreams and start celebrating your success! My mission is to share this and expand globally.

Will you join me in this mission? Please share this book and planner with your friends and family. It's a simple request. Let's spread the news to the people who you care most about and show them how easy it is to Create The Perfect Day!

A Few Experiences in Creating the Perfect Day

I had a goal when I set out to write *Create The Perfect Day* and its companion *Create The Perfect Day Planner*. I wanted to impact the life of at least one person by sharing the system I created.

As is often the case, I selected a few colleagues and friends to read and review both Create the Perfect Day book and the Planner in draft form before they were published.

My goal was to gain feedback about the system and how easy it is to implement and how well it adapts to different needs and personalities. Here are a few of the results and the stories they shared!

Mary's Story

Let me tell you about my friend. I am going to call her Mary. I asked Mary to read Create The Perfect Day and tell me what she thought.

After giving her time to read the book, we spoke on the phone. I was concerned because the first thing she did was start to cry! Then she explained that they were tears of joy; that she had not only read *Create The Perfect Day*, she went through the process and implemented the steps!

Her tears were because it had brought her husband herself closer, strengthened their marriage, and saved a family.

This was not what I had expected!

My mission was to impact at least one life with *Create The Perfect Day*. I smiled as I realized it was already making an impact.

Mary's story fuels my passion to help many others on a global basis.

Gordon's Story

Here's a story from a client of mine named Gordon who also was asked to review the book and planner.

I was fortunate to cross paths with Jessica Peterson," Gordon said, "who is an amazing leader and just a down right great person. Throughout our working relationship, Jessica has enlightened me, and helped guide me down the right path with my business.

As someone that has always struggled with time management, I found her book to be very helpful. The question and answer portion of the book made it easy for me to focus on what really matters to me, and to break it down into daily segments, rather than just broad goals.

Planning out my perfect day was fun. It allowed me to look at what is really important to me, and to focus on all of the things in life that I enjoy.

The format of the planner, including daily gratitude, actions, and celebrating our successes, is incredible.

I highly recommend connecting with Jessica and using her *Create The Perfect Day* system.

Logan's Story

And here is another reviewer's experience, shared by Logan Hall, the founder of GenZ.

I felt, as a reader, that I left with something I could see. You walk your reader through processes, you're not just spewing content.

Most books in this genre are only out there so readers can know the author's thoughts or philosophies. Most, no matter how they deny it, simply are sharing a thought or idea.

This is not a bad thing, but often times the reader simply forgets or puts it out of their mind not long after finishing the book.

This book is different in that it includes a process with actions to be followed! And a planner to keep on creating that perfect day over and over again!

Introducing
Create The Perfect Day™ System

I commend you for taking steps to make the most out of life.

This book introduces my *Create The Perfect Day™* process and is designed to be most effective when used together with the *Create The Perfect Day Planner*. The system introduced in this book and implemented in the planner is based on YOUR dreams and goals.

This book is guaranteed to share the following with you:

Focus and Balance

First to discuss the four focus areas to balance for happiness in life. This was based on a conversation with a retired neuro surgeon whom I highly admire, on trial and error, and my own readings and research. There are spaces for you to write in your answer to thought-provoking questions. There are no right or wrong answers. Use this book to take action; fill in the blanks and start creating the perfect day. We are here to deliver insight, questions, and information.

Dream BIG

Second, we will dive into the bigger picture. My mission is to ask you questions that will get you started dreaming BIG. We will share a simple and effective way to create a digital dream big board that you can take with you wherever you go.

Planning and Action

Third, we will go through a vital step, plan, and act sequence. We call this the *Let's Plan It and Take Action Series.* Yahoo!

Create The Perfect Day

Fourth, we will take you on the exciting journey of creating the perfect day. My clients have had so much fun going on this journey. Each day will look different. For example, my perfect day on Mondays involves walking the beach and going on a lunch date with my husband.

Our action guide will start with simple questions such as, when you wake up what is the first thing you hear, smell, hear and see? It has been so much fun to hear what my clients have said. Some say they wake up seeing their dog and smell their coffee brewing because they pressed a remote control to start it. Another said I wake up seeing these beautiful curtains and realized I don't have them, so I am going to buy them! I have even heard I wake up seeing the ocean, and it is not there. So now they can take steps to make it happen!

Consistent and Productive

Fifth, we will bring all of this together and plan your perfect days, Monday to Sunday. This will guide you to be productive and protective of your time.

Celebrate

Sixth, we will take you on a journey to discover ways to celebrate the small and big accomplishments in your life. So often we take what we have accomplished and forget to celebrate. It can cause us to lose the joy that we all deserve

Share the Wealth

Seventh, we ask you to share this with a friend. Our mission is to impact at least one million lives and we need your support to make this happen.

The process you will learn in *Create The Perfect Day* works very well with our *Create The Perfect Day Planner* and with digital schedulers such as Google Calendar and Outlook Calendar. They are not required or necessary.

This book is the first step to *Create The Perfect Day*. Congrats on having it!

Brief Story on How This Came About

Have you ever had an "aha" moment where everything came clear? That is what happened to me and inspired me to write this book. Before I explain more, please allow me to share a little bit about myself and how this moment came about.

I'm a speaker, author, consultant, coach, wife, mom, and a big advocate for volunteering. My company has evolved and grown. It began as Customer WOW Project for five years and now is Simply WOW Agency. My favorite quote is, "Keep It Simple."

During a successful banking, mortgage and insurance career spanning two decades, people asked me how I was able to be top in sales and a top employee. My response was simple: to first truly care for people. I remember one sales person I said this to who did not like my response. This made me sad; when you truly care for people, you have the best foundation.

Then I was introduced to social media. My excitement for it was high. What a great way to stay in touch with people! Every person I meet in my personal and business life who I admire, I can now connect with and stay in touch. Social media goes above and beyond just an email or even a phone call. It saves time and allows me to focus on people, which is what being in a customer service business is all about; it's the people who matter most.

After several years of testing social media, I came up with a formula that has brought success to me and to others with whom I've shared it. As a matter of fact, one of my clients recently reported a success she directly attributes to my formula! She had, over a decade in business, acquired a few sales representatives in her business. After my training, she had—in three months—increased the number of sales representatives to over 200.

That got me to say WOW!

My secret is simple: WOW people, your business will grow, and you will have a prosperous life.

In my agency, we consult and coach on over 50 topics. The list is actively growing, however here are the five top subjects our clients ask for:

- Social Media (aka Social WOW),
- Productivity and Business Planning,
- Networking,
- Offline Marketing,
- Systems.

Balance is Key and Essential;
Not Always Easy.

O ver the years people say I'm driven and inspiring. Each day I look
at myself as another human being with a drive to see people happy.

One day I was sitting at a Gary Barnes International Conference.
I was one of his speakers on social media.

The moment hit me when I realized if we each save one hour a day, and multiply that times 365 days in a year, then divide that by a 40-hour work week, it equals nine weeks.

WOW!

I realized every person who saves one hour out of their day is essentially gifting themselves nine weeks of time off.

Can you imagine what you would do with that time? Imagine how much more happiness there would be. I started imagining how people could spend time with families, volunteer more, go laugh with friends more often, and travel. How much more happiness there would be! Intriguing, isn't it? (If you'd like to know more, find **9 Weeks Off**, the book I co-authored here: http://www.9WeeksOf.com. This book dives into ways to save time and have more time.)

Then the day came my husband ended up in ICU.

We had just moved from Colorado to Florida. My husband's dad passed away in December. Then a friend of ours who we highly admire and had partnered with in business passed away in December. It was a hard month.

In January, my husband came to me and said, "We are moving to Florida, I bought a house."

My thoughts were, *You did what?*

We had been married that month for 18 years and my husband has never done anything like that! Our dream was to move to Florida, and we were planning on it, just not that quick!

He gave me thirty days. The good news is he was able to get out of buying the house (the seller changed their mind on selling, whew!), but we still set out to move to Florida.

It was a hard adjustment at first. I missed my friends and family dearly. My kid was in fifth grade and left all her friends.

Exactly three months after being in Florida, I had my first local speaking engagement. I was super pumped up because the Founder was someone I admired, and the people were great! It was my time to deliver some value to people in my own community.

The next day I woke up with my husband leaning right over my face asking if his eyes were ok. As I attempted to wake up and look, I said, "Yes. Why do you ask?"

"I am not able to see well," was his response.

My husband, Evan, is not one to visit doctors often. We both recognized that something was wrong, and I started calling around to get him into an eye doctor. Nobody would see him. They said he needed to go into the Emergency Room. Then I remembered that I'd recently met several people who had detached retinas. That scared us both because if that is the case you have to get attention ASAP!

We decided to go the Emergency Room. We are sitting there in the waiting area, thinking detached retina, not even a glimmer of the devastating news we would receive.

When the doctor's first saw Evan, the thought was that he was having a stroke. After testing, the doctors came back to say he has two masses on his brainstem.

My heart sank! I had no family here. I left Evan for a bit and went to the car. I started to cry, and cry hard (this was huge because I rarely cry). I thought how can this be???

When I went back in to the hospital, friends whom we recently met at our place of worship came and visited. They were helpful and uplifting. Then we were asked about medical directives. It is a good thing we had one. Most people do not, and I highly suggest you do.

The next thing I knew he was admitted to the Intensive Care Unit. I kept asking for answers. Nobody would give me any.

There was a small waiting room for people there to visit loved ones in ICU. I remember one family that was facing losing their son who was barely out of high school. It broke my heart. So young! Then I realized my husband is still young as well; almost 40!

I sat there alone; looked around and everyone had someone. The good news about having very tough moments in my life, including when my mother tried to take her life, helped me to be able to face moments like these. You could say it toughened me up. I speak a bit further about it in the book *Purpose Powered People*.

Finally, after gaining security clearance, I was able to go in and see my husband. We kept demanding answers. We got some. He was high risk for not making it, due to the bleeding on his brain. A neuro surgeon advised us that the bleeding was in the worst spot possible; in the brainstem and deep inside the brainstem.

That month was extremely difficult. Apparently, the stress was too much for me and I did not realize it. I drove myself to urgent care. The one side of my face did not look right. The doctor informed me I had Bell's Palsy.

To this day there have been many other challenges, including a family member in a coma and some dear friends killed in a hotel fire. I share this to let you know that no matter what you are going through, please remember to hang in there and get through it. Better days are ahead. Life has its moments; ups and downs.

My Aha! Moment

I am not a person to focus on everything that goes wrong, but in the past year, I have realized how short life is! My aha moment came not in an instant, but over time. Deep down inside I felt this calling to share what I know about creating the perfect day.

I've taught this concept for some time to my clients and perfected the system to implement creating the perfect day. And then one day I realized that something amazing was happening. Some of my clients, those who embraced a combination of several of my trainings were finding immense personal and professional success and balance in their lives. As I thought about this, I realized that these clients all embraced a unique combination of my training systems: Being Balanced, Dream Big Digital Board, and Creating the Perfect Day Planning and Productivity.

These clients created their perfect day and fell in love with the process. They started living!

It truly was an Aha! Moment and I reflected on how this system had come to be. I went way back to playing as a kid and the passion I had to make sure my Barbie dolls were fashionable, career girls who also volunteered. I loved to write out their schedules and plan when they got raises. That innocent play was a big indicator at that moment as to what my calling in life was to be. Even as a child I imagined the perfect day.

I reflected on what I love about coaching my clients. It's having them light up with joy in having created a day-to-day plan to live their life to the full!

To educate my clients about how to create strong relationships with people was also high on my list of what I love to do.

I realized that I coach on more than social media and creating results. I coach people on how to create their days based on their dreams and goals, on how to have what they want, desire, and deserve.

Then I reflected that there is a limit to how many people I can serve directly. And that deep-down calling, that aha moment became huge. I felt this BIG calling to share the book and planner *Create The Perfect Day*.

I realized that once people CREATE it, they LIVE and LOVE their days.

Create a life you desire.

Increase productivity.

Be happy.

My BIG Dream is for YOU

My BIG dream is to hear how this book has changed people's lives.

Yes, that is YOU!

I want to hear that you are now balanced, happier, going after big dreams, and creating a life that you desire. My goal is to have you be IN-SPIRED and to take ACTION.

Are you ready to start creating your perfect day? Great! We will make it simple and fun. You will fall in love and start living it! Let's get started; grab your pen and let's have fun!

Your Purpose or Why

This brief chapter is going to discuss your purpose; your reason for doing; your *why*. If you do not know your purpose right now, that is ok! In due time, it will become clear to you.

There are books and companies who offer services to help you discover your purpose. Some believe taking personality tests reveal more information and benefit them. It is a good idea to reflect upon your purpose and to be in touch with your why.

Recently I poised the question on social media asking, "How do you know your purpose?" It was wonderful to hear the responses from my friends. Quite a few shared their personal purpose. Here are some of the responses:

When you have a day that made you happy.

It's what gets you out of bed with excitement!

When you find your gift and share it, then you know your purpose.

Personally, I have enjoyed asking people what they loved to do as a kid. There is a big link with your passion as a kid to your purpose. I have a friend who feels her childhood has held her back from really realizing her purpose. The good news is your purpose can be discovered (and rediscovered!) anytime—there's no expiration date.

Recently I watched a wonderful video of a gentleman who lost his wife. After being married many years, he felt like he had no purpose anymore. A little girl came approached him at the grocery store and changed his life. Every week that little girl and her mom get together with him. He says he now has purpose.

I share this with you because your purpose can change. Life is evolving. Evolve with it.

When you know your purpose, it is much easier to *Create The Perfect Day*.

Four Essential Parts to a Perfect Day

When we look at life, there are four simple and essential parts to maximize the perfect day. Each are equally important. A friend of mine, Dr Dylaan once said that our life is like a car. When we have one flat tire, it is more challenging to get where we want. When we look at these four steps, if we miss one, it takes longer to get where we desire.

Health, Wealth, Relationships, and Social Impact (which includes spiritual and moral values). Each of these parts are essential to a perfect day.

When we are off balance in one area, it can make it more challenging to get to where you want to go. By focusing on all four essential parts to a perfect day, we achieve more and find it easier to enjoy our day-to-day life.

Health

The stronger our health is the better our life is. Every person has unique challenges around health.

Wealth

Wealth can come in a variety of ways. For some wealth means buying a home, or more homes. For others, wealth may mean investing, or perhaps having a business or an increased income in their company. It's important to keep our mindset around wealth in balance with the other three parts. A focus on lack or acquisition can pull attention away from the other parts.

Relationships

We were created to give and receive love. Relationships are essential to designing our perfect days. Relationships can grow or expand in a variety of ways. For some. Relationships are centered around family. You may choose to dedicate more time to your partner, spouse, or children. Others may desire to find true love. Companies may desire to grow their business relationships. Your wants around relationship may also involve expanding or finding your tribe of friends.

Social Impact (spiritual and moral value)

Social impact and moral values ultimately strengthen our lives and communities. The more you can develop your values and make a difference, the better your days will be. There is more happiness in giving than receiving. Do be open to receiving! For some this can be faith based; others it may be volunteering

Are you ready to get into action and work on the perfect day?

In *Create The Perfect Day Planner*, we ask you to review each of these essential parts every week. Later in this book, we gift you a sample week from the actual *Create The Perfect Day Planner* so that you can experience creating the perfect day now.

Understanding how interconnected each part is to the other is important when looking at how to implement balance between these four essentials. The focus is on action. And that begins by reviewing and acting on each part, every week.

For each part, the planner asks you to:

- Set goals

- Express why achieving the goal is important to you

- Define one action to implement.

Fill in your answers to the questions posed in each four essential parts.

Health
What goals do you have with your health?
Why is this important to you?
What is one action you can implement over the next 30-90 days?

Wealth

What goals do you have financially?

Why is this important to you?

What is one action you can implement over the next 30-90 days?

Relationships

What goals do you have when it comes to relationships?

Why is this important to you?

What is one action you can implement over the next 30-90 days?

Social Impact, Moral Value

What areas can you work on improving in your life that will benefit you and others?

Why is this important to you?

What is one action you can implement over the next 30-90 days?

Congratulations on completing your first action!

Dream Big

Are you ready to now start dreaming big? Fantastic!

Now that we understand the four essentials, let's move on over to expanding on your dreams and creating the perfect day.

What does dreaming big look like to you?

Some have said they would like to expand on their dreams in life. Others desire clarity on what their dreams are.

Your Dream Big Board

This is your time to sit back and have fun! The Dream Big Board action is designed for you to simply answer questions and create visuals from those answers. The result is that you create a board with visuals that will inspire you every day.

Our favorite way of creating a dream big board is by using social media. There is one channel where you can easily create a board and take it with you for daily inspiration.

The social media channel to use and take your dream big board with you anywhere is Pinterest. You may wonder, "How is that so?"

Great question! Here is a simple way to create your dream big board.

First, you will need a Pinterest account.

Second, create a new board on Pinterest.

Give it any title you like and set it to either private or public, depending on if you want to share your vision with others. I call mine Dream Big, others may call their Dream Life, or Inspiration board. You can name it whatever you desire.

Third step is to complete the Dream Big form.

Once you complete the form, look for visuals to match your answers. You can type in certain words or phrases in the Pinterest search bar. When you find an image you like, you can pin it.

Another great choice is to upload a photo onto Pinterest and save it to your board.

Bonus:

It is highly suggested you place the Pinterest app on your phone. This will enable you to check in daily and be inspired, along with being reminded about your dreams!

Dream Big Action

Whom are you surrounded with? What influence do you have?

What emotions or feelings do you want to experience in your day?

Are there hobbies you would like to start or continue?

Your love life. What does that look like to you?

Where do you want to live? What do you desire your home to look like?

Where would you like to travel?

What book(s) would you like to read?

What clubs, organizations or masterminds will you join?

Investments you desire to make?

Will you journal or write? About what topic?

What health goals do you have?

New habits you like to create?

What ways can you volunteer or serve more?

What income would you like to GET?

What would you like to achieve in your business or career?

What will you do to celebrate life?

Reflect Daily on Your Vision

Now that you have completed your Dream BIG Action, the next step is to create a physical board or binder with pictures.

Our favorite method is the Pinterest way, mentioned above, which makes it easy to see and change your vision board anytime. Many like the solidity of cut out pictures; if you are crafty and prefer this method, go for it! The process should fit your world, your life, your personality.

The purpose of the Dream BIG Action is for you to create something that you can reflect on daily and that will inspire you to take action!

A Gift For You

And once you have created your Dream BIG vision board, share the good news. Share the hashtag #createtheperfectday on your social media. Then join our Facebook community and write a post telling us where you shared the news. We will happily send you a digital version of *Create The Day Planner* as gift to celebrate!

GET™ Statements

Our Dream BIG system is a fantastic tool for visualizing what you want. There's also a secret formula (called GET Statements) for GETTING what you want that we highly recommend. A GET Statement is a great companion to dreaming BIG and setting goals.

Gary Barnes is the creator of GET Statements. I'm one of his few GET Statement coaches. As a certified GET Statement Coach and graduate of the 100k Impact Business Coaching program, I work with people teaching them the GET Statement formula.

If this interests you, please visit garybarnesinternational.com or connect with me at simplywowagency.com.

What Can Hold You Back

Do you have fears?

I do. Over the years I've discovered that all people have fears. It is ok to have fears. It can actually protect us. Fear tells us we are in danger. Sometimes, though, it is imagined, not real.

We often think things are going to be hard and then are pleasantly surprised when they are not. When it comes to creating the perfect day, there are real fears that can hinder us and prevent our creating days we love.

I have heard some say these are reasons that prevent us from being all we desire, some of the fears we let stand in our way:

- Fear of success
- What if I fail
- Do I deserve it
- Low confidence to make it happen
- Feel alone
- Lost on next steps

Here is an affirmation for you:

I deserve, expect, and receive the perfect day.

It is vital you take the time to reflect on what can prevent you from creating the perfect day. Write out what feelings you have. The goal is to overcome your challenges and conquer through the next phase; planning.

Create the Perfect Day in Business

When I've worked with business owners in business planning, goal setting, and productivity, there have been moments where we discovered major flaws in creating the perfect day in business. It brings me so much joy when my clients have that heavy feeling in their life and business lifted off and taken away. They say the feeling of a hamster in a cage is taken away.

What I've learned, and was there myself at one time, is we just go and go in our business without a clear plan or vision. We are basically hopping on the hamster wheel and getting nowhere. A business owner can feel frustrated, tired, and worn out.

This week I had a business owner who came to me wanting guidance on creating a plan to success. My first question was "What is your BIG vision for your company?"

He said "That is a really good question. I do not even know!"

You see, since he did not know, then there is no way he can get anywhere.

If you are someone who does not know where you want to go or be, then that is ok. We have walked through with business owners and discussed what they really want and desire; their BIG vision. Your vision may change as well. Please know that is ok. What a beautiful gift we have of life and are here to make the most of it. It makes me sad when people stay where they are at in misery, not even making the smallest of changes to go where they really desire.

Some business owners want to make more money. Commonly I hear how much they would like to make. When I dive into mapping out how much they make per client and their sales process, we typically find major flaws. The good news is we map it out to where they can and will earn the money they desire.

Once we figure out the BIG vision and map out what is necessary to get there, we break it down into goals. That is one of the big reasons I developed the *Create The Perfect Day Planner* as a 30 and 90 day system not only is it wonderful for personal goals, but also for business goals.

Once we have the goals set, we create the steps to achieve the goal. We are clear on how much time, when and where to invest time.

This week I received a message from a past client. It made me so happy to hear from him! As a matter of fact, in one day I received three messages from clients who mentioned how grateful they were for my help in their business and life. It made me happy! This past client mentioned how he was grateful for the business and life plan. He is working on following his perfect day system and is beyond ecstatic for it. He was very stressed at one point in time and now he is much calmer and moving ahead in his success.

When you are creating the perfect day for your personal life please also include information on creating the perfect day in your business.

I do offer a simple 6 Figure WOW Blueprint that can be used to identify where you want to go with your business. It's available from www.simply-wowagency.com. Feel free to go grab it!

Let's Plan It!

So often people get wrapped up in day-to-day life. The list seems never ending! The good news is this plan will deliver more clarity and happiness in creating your perfect days.

The next step is to write out goals based around what you've done thus far.

What goals will you create around each of the four essential steps and your dream big board? Now is the time to start writing it out!

After you complete this activity, we are going to start an activity that my clients over the years love. We will dive into each day of the week and incorporate your goals and dreams. When you plan it, fall in love with it and then act to start living it. That is why we say: Create a life you desire. Increase productivity. Be happy.

Perfect Day Action Sheet

Now that your goals are set, let's dive into the little but powerful details in a day.

Please take at least 10 minutes to complete the Perfect Day action sheet that follows over the next several pages. Every person has a different idea on what the perfect day is and this exercise allows you to brainstorm and begin to visualize what YOUR perfect day looks like.

Ok, you ready? Remember, have fun. Creating your perfect day should be enjoyable and help you to realize the possibility of it becoming reality.

This action adds new ideas and thoughts into your perfect day. It is an easy step by step action sheet. Let's get started!

Perfect Day Action Sheet

When you first wake up in the morning, what do you hear? Birds? Ocean? Kids? Or pure silence? Describe this in enough detail to bring it mind every time you read it.

When you open your eyes first thing in the morning, what do you see? What are the colors of your walls? What is the layout of your room?

Where are you located at? Are you in a certain location?

Who else is in the room with you? What time is it? Do you feel the sun or look out at snow?

When you get out of bed, are you jumping with joy or do you decide to hang out there for a bit?

When you stand up, what is the first thing you will do?

What is the perfect breakfast in the morning? Walk to the kitchen, what does your house look like?

What adventure or plans do you have for the day? Does it vary depending on the day of the week?

Do you start your day with a routine? What does that look like? Read, pray, silence, stretch, visualize, affirmations, work out, journal, talk with a friend or family, walk, or something else?

What comes next in your day? Is it having the perfect breakfast?

What do you smell? What do you feel throughout your day? Is it the smell of your kids? The beach? Mountain fresh air? Hug your pet? Flowers?

Do you work-out? Go volunteer? Work?

What are the perfect food or meals you take in?

Are there events you go to? Places you visit on a regular basis?

What is your favorite hobby? Have you made time for it?

Do you visualize your passions and dreams daily? What does your journal or writing spot look like?

What activity do you find yourself doing that you lose track of the clock because you love it so much?

Or is out having lunch everyday with 1 friend. What is your conversation about and whom are you with?

Maybe you go on your boat? Out fishing? Or sewing? Feeding homeless? Building a home? Taking a class? These are only ideas, there are endless possibilities.

Anything holding you back from having your perfect day? What is it? What can you do to change it?

How do you want your family and friends to remember you? Do your daily activities reflect it?

Now that you have your first perfect day down, are you ready to write out your second perfect day and your third? The perfect days can be endless. Now is the time to write out your desires for each day of the week.

Monday:

Tuesday:

Wednesday:

Thursday:

Friday:

Saturday:

Sunday:

Last but Not Least

Thus far, we have focused on the daily actions we take to live and love our life. There are also thirty-day and ninety-day goals we set.

Goals provide you with clarity about which direction to go. Often our minds do not listen to our hearts. The process of projecting goals into the next 30 and 90 days often makes it apparent that there is a gap between what we desire and what we *think* we desire. Let's start your journey to what you desire to create in thirty days.

What is your BIG Goal to achieve in the next 30 or 90 days?

What are the action steps to achieve your BIG Goal?

Why do you deserve to achieve this goal?

What good will be created with your BIG Goal?

Who will hold you accountable?

Now that you have your four essential parts to being balanced, your DREAM Big board, perfect day, daily activities, and BIG goal with steps to accomplish, it is time to start adding it to your *Create The Perfect Day Planner*.

Here is a sample of a week in our *Create The Perfect Day Planner*. You can take your daily activities and incorporate them. It may be your job, taking kids to school, going to the gym, or reading.

Some may say that their job is not ideal for their perfect day. Do put it in the allotted slots BUT start filling in the other time slots with action for you to leave your job if that is your dream!

We so often dream and never write it out or create a dream big board around it to be inspired. You now have taken that important and vital step. The final one is to plan it and act! Without action, it is unlikely to happen. Your life will control you instead of you taking charge of it.

You will see a schedule starting at 4 A.M and ending at 11 P.M. Each day will look different. Start time blocking based on your goals and actions.

Life will have changes. Your goals and dreams will change. That is ok! You can go ahead and add or delete to your digital dream big board. You can alter your perfect days. The purpose is to keep you inspired, focused, and taking action to make it happen.

There are some days people have as empty space in their time. That is great! You just never know what may come that day for you to take care of. Having empty space can be a good thing. Please allow those extra times to do whatever may come your way or that you are inclined to do. Sometimes it may not need to be so detailed. For example, you may have time blocked to be with family. The activities do not necessarily have to be scheduled; just the time with them.

Enjoy this and start taking what you have dreamed and planned; add it into your life!

Create The Perfect Day™ Planner

After exploring all the planners out there, none fit my needs and my clients. That's when I was determined to CREATE one.

Create The Perfect Day Planner starts out with journaling. It is powerful and healing for the soul to journal.

Under the Journal is a section for notes. Do you have an idea or something to jot down and don't want to forget? This is the area for it. You can even draw if your heart desires!

In the *Create The Perfect Day Planner* you will note an action section. This is where you place what you have or need to do for that day. Instead of saying to do, the word action is more appealing. You are more likely to be excited to accomplish it. We also say take out the words have to and replace with want to. When you do so, it shifts our outlook on our day. Remember, if there is something you do not like, then create goals and take action to start making changes!

Each day starts out with one intention. When we set our heart to accomplish one thing per day, our chances of success increase.

You will see a section stating, "Today I look forward to". This small statement is powerful and will make an impact on your perfect days!

Next to each day you will be asked to write down what you are grateful for that day. Gratitude is very important and to reflect on it. Are you up to make it a goal and write out at least three things you are grateful for?

Every week in our *Create The Perfect Day Planner*, we have at the beginning what goals you are set to accomplish. There is a slot on what will you do to celebrate the success!

Every thirty to ninety days in the *Create The Perfect Day Planner*, there is a spot to set your big goals and action steps. You can schedule it to make it happen. You will be asked how will you celebrate when accomplishing them. At the end of thirty or ninety days, there will be a review section. Time to reflect back and look for ways to improve.

How Do I Get the Planner?

A one-week version of *Create The Perfect Day Planner* is shared below. Many of you have expressed a desire to have a complete digital or printed *Create The Perfect Day Planner* to utilize. Check out our *Create The Perfect Day Planner* packages at www.createtheperfectday.com

"Your work is going to fill a large part of your life, and the only way to be truly satisfied is to do what you believe is great work. And the only way to do great work is to love what you do. If you haven't found it yet, keep looking. Don't settle. As with all matters of the heart, you'll know when you find it."

~ Steve Jobs

Begin with... Assessment & Action

Please define your purpose: (Hint: What makes you happy? What gifts/talents do you share?)

What is the one BIG goal you would like to achieve in 30 or 90 days?

What fear do you have and how will you overcome it?

Why do you deserve to achieve this?

What good will be created in the world by you achieving this?

What are your action steps to accomplish the one BIG goal?

Who will hold you accountable?

How will you celebrate when you achieve the one big goal?

Next, let's schedule it! You can do this on your planner here and/or digitally. Plan it and Act on it.

To Achieve Balance

In Create The Perfect Day action book, we discuss four essential focus areas to get balanced. In this section, please take time to write down your goal in each area.

Health

The stronger our health is the better our life is. Every person has their own unique goals. Each goal has a reason behind it. Your action is to write out your goals for your health and why it is important.

What goals do you have with your health?

Why is this important to you?

What is one action you can implement over the next 30-90 days?

Wealth

Wealth can come in a variety of ways. For some it is to buy a home or more homes. Others it may to start investing. Some it may be to start a business or increase income in their company

What goals do you have financially?

Why is this important to you?

What is one action you can implement over the next 30-90 days?

Relationships

We were created to give and receive love. Relationships are essential to our perfect days. Relation-ships can grow or expand in a variety of ways. For some it is to dedicate more time to their partners, spouse or children. Some may desire to find true love. Companies may desire to grow their business relation-ships. Some want to expand and find their tribe of friends.

What goals do you have when it comes to relationships?

Why is this important to you?

What is one action you can implement over the next 30-90 days?

Social Impact, Moral Value

Social impact and moral values ultimately strengthen our lives and communities. The more you can develop in your values and make a difference, the better your days will be. There is more happiness in giving than receiving. Do be open to receiving! For some this can be faith based; others it may be volunteering more.

What areas can you work on improving in your life that will benefit you and others?

Why is this important to you?

What is one action you can implement over the next 30-90 days?

In Create The Perfect Day action book we also had you dive deep into your dreams and visualizing the smaller details in your perfect day. Now is the time to incorporate those!

Daily Action

Do you have regular action on certain days of the week? In Create The Perfect Day action book we discussed creating the perfect day for weekdays.

What action do you desire to create and act on each day?

Write out what action you desire on each day of the week.

Monday:

Tuesday:

Wednesday:

Thursday:

Friday:

Saturday:

Sunday:

Take Action

This week what do you desire to achieve?

How will you celebrate your success?

What challenges could you face?

How do you plan to overcome it and achieve the perfect day?

Events this week:

Inspiring Quote:

Journal:

Notes:

Monday...

Daily Action

Inspiring Quote:

Journal:

Notes:

Daily Action Plan

Today, I look forward to:

Actions

4 am

5

6

7

8

9

10

11

12

1

2

3

4

5

6

7

8

9

10

11 pm

What am I most grateful for today?

Tuesday...　　　Daily Action

Inspiring Quote:

Journal:

Notes:

Daily Action Plan

Today, I look forward to:

Actions

4 am

5

6

7

8

9

10

11

12

1

2

3

4

5

6

7

8

9

10

11 pm

What am I most grateful for today?

Daily Action

Inspiring Quote:

Journal:

Notes:

Daily Action Plan

Today, I look forward to: (Date)

Actions

4 am

5

6

7

8

9

10

11

12

1

2

3

4

5

6

7

8

9

10

11 pm

What am I most grateful for today?

Thursday...

Daily Action

Inspiring Quote:

Journal:

Notes:

Daily Action Plan

Today, I look forward to:

Actions

4 am

5

6

7

8

9

10

11

12

1

2

3

4

5

6

7

8

9

10

11 pm

What am I most grateful for today?

Daily Action

Inspiring Quote:

Journal:

Notes:

Daily Action Plan

Today, I look forward to:

Actions

4 am

5

6

7

8

9

10

11

12

1

2

3

4

5

6

7

8

9

10

11 pm

What am I most grateful for today?

Daily Action

Inspiring Quote:

Journal:

Notes:

Daily Action Plan

Today, I look forward to:

Actions

4 am

5

6

7

8

9

10

11

12

1

2

3

4

5

6

7

8

9

10

11 pm

What am I most grateful for today?

Inspiring Quote:

Journal:

Notes:

Daily Action Plan

Today, I look forward to: (Date)

Actions

4 am

5

6

7

8

9

10

11

12

1

2

3

4

5

6

7

8

9

10

11 pm

What am I most grateful for today?

Review Your Week

Wow! Another fantastic week went by. What awesomeness did you create?

What did you learn this past week?

We hope you enjoyed this full-featured version of *Create The Perfect Day Planner*. It's included here as our gift to get you started on your journey to *Create The Perfect Day*.

Remember, a complete digital or printed version of the planner is available. Order from Amazon.com or at www.createtheperfectday.com

Time to Celebrate!

Celebrate

You have set out to accomplish your goals and dreams, let's plan how you will celebrate! Are you someone who does not celebrate much, big or small wins in life? Today I am giving you permission to start celebrating. You deserve to!

I did not always celebrate. The importance came to me recently. When life changed so dramatically with my husband's diagnosis, I was inspired my friend and coach who looked for the happiness and joy in life. Now I teach others how to celebrate.

Here you will be inspired on new ideas and ways to celebrate small or big accomplishments. This goes very well with the *Create The Perfect Day Planner*. When you set out goals, you write down how you will celebrate when accomplishing it. There will be more information about our *Create The Perfect Day Planner* right after you come up with some fun ways to celebrate! Are you ready to be inspired and have some ideas on how to celebrate? Let's go!

Let's Celebrate!

Create a top list of restaurants to go visit for breakfast, lunch, and dinner. For example, say you set a goal to connect with 10 people and deliver value—and you've accomplished it. Go celebrate! Invite someone to join you and make it 11 connections!

Invest in yourself. Maybe a massage, chiropractor visit, spa treatment, pedicure or nails. Set a goal with the intention to celebrate its completion. Investing in yourself takes away guilt and shifts mindset to accomplishment!

I am a big fan of giving back. When you accomplish a financial goal, donate a set amount to your favorite charity or charities. If this really fuels you, then set this intention and celebrate by giving back! What financial goal will you accomplish? What charity will you give to? And how much?

Sometimes celebrating can even be as simple as sharing it with someone you cherish or love. What a great feeling to connect with a person and share it. Listen to their successes as well and encourage them. Who would you love to connect with?

You may prefer to shop as a reward. Nothing is wrong with that. Keep in mind to be specific and set a budget. For example, once you close a certain amount in business, then you will buy a new pair of shoes up to a certain amount. Then go have fun! Oh, and if you discover something else you desire or want, add it to your celebration list! What items do you desire? What financial goals will you set for yourself to buy them?

What if you want to go on vacation? This may be on your dream big board. Set your goals and what you want to accomplish to achieve that trip. Great incentive!

Sometimes it can also be as simple as a bubble bath and reading. Daily reading is highly suggested to be a part of every person's perfect day. A way to celebrate may be extra reading. If you are a lover of wisdom, once you achieve a certain goal you might celebrate by visiting a local or online book store to buy a book that you have desired.

Do you love fresh flowers? We are big fan of paying it forward. How about you celebrate by buying yourself and a friend flowers? A priceless investment is in relationships. What are your favorite flowers and what will you accomplish to buy them? Which friends would you like to surprise with flowers?

There are moments to celebrate with a movie you know is coming out. Is this a way you like to celebrate?

Perhaps you are a game lover. You can stroll online to see what new games are out there and set a goal to celebrate with buying one. Board games are wonderful because you can have friends over and have fun! What games would you like to buy?

What musical instrument would you like to have? Or maybe a new techy gadget?

What new hobbies will you invest in?

How about throwing a party? Gives a reason to share the good news of what you have accomplished with your friends!

There are big ways to celebrate. Do you desire a new boat, home, car, or jewelry?

I believe every person should set time limits on social media. How about extra time on social media-outside as a reward?

Celebrate at your favorite winery or pub?

What about a new outfit? Cruise online and be inspired by one.

Go laugh with friends on the playground and swing!

Animals put a smile on so many people's faces. What are your favorite animal spots to go visit? Or maybe the local Aquarium?

There are countless ways to celebrate. What is your favorite way to celebrate?

Live The Perfect Day—Every Day

Are you ready to truly start creating, living and loving your days? A BIG component to making it happen is to utilize an important tool: *Create The Perfect Day Planner.* A variety of packages are available at www.createtheperfectday.com

Thank you for reading *Create The Perfect Day.*

Please visit our private Facebook group at

https://www.facebook.com/groups/createtheperfectday/

to interact with others who are ready to Create The Perfect Day!

If you enjoyed this book, please share it on social media and with your friends in conversations. We want them to thank you and we thank you as well!

Please do tag us in your posts. When we see your tag, we will respond and give you a digital copy of the book to share with someone else.

About the Author

Jessica Peterson is the Founder of the Simply WOW Agency and Customer WOW Project. She often shares how, even as a young girl, her Barbie had a career and volunteered. Their schedule and finances were mapped out. Committed to life-long learning, Jessica has a passion for numbers and simplifying processes. This is no surprise because she excelled and skipped ahead in math courses at school.

Jessica's background is banking, mortgage and financial/insurance. She constantly won top sales and employee.

As an author, Jessica has five books currently available. *Purpose Powered People, Forty and Wiser: Remarkable Insider Secrets from Women 40 and Wiser*, and the previously mentioned *Entrepreneurs: Instantly Create 9 Weeks of Time Off!* are the three most recent.

She is one of the Founders of Contractor Success Training and Mortgage Prosperity Academy.

Jessica guides Simply WOW Agency to serve these industries:

- Coaches
- Mortgage Professionals
- Real Estate Agents and Agencies
- Insurance Professionals
- Financial Advisors
- Contractors
- Companies who have innovative solutions to serve and positively impact lives

Connect with Jessica

Website: http://www.simplywowagency.com

Facebook: https://www.facebook.com/simplywowagency

LinkedIn: https://www.linkedin.com/in/jessicasimplywow/

Acknowledgment

Grateful for CaZ at Manifest Publishing. Not only is CaZ amazing at editing a book and planner, she also has wonderful insight into the look and feel. CaZ also saved me from making a big mistake that many authors do, that would have hindered the planner being accessible to the world and making less of an impact.

Thank you CaZ for having a part in making a difference in lives not only for this book and planner but also with your other clients

Kudos for the Book and Planner

"I loved Create The Perfect Day*! I know I'm a bit emotional, but I cried trying to answer the questions about my future, and then it helped me to organize my life. I read it with my husband and we both are going to make changes to have that Perfect Day!!*

That's a fantastic read!!"

~ Sonya McNair

"When you go from good to great, you need a strategy. Create The Perfect Day *provides you with a strategy on how to go above and beyond. The steps outlined in Jessica's book will make you a great author, business coach, speaker, service provider, contractor, or whatever your field may be. This guidebook will give you the steps to plan your perfect day and space to write down all your strategies in order to accomplish what you aim for. Go BIG! Take the leap of faith by purchasing this book to learn the step by step strategy to go from good to great!"*

~ Storm Pierce

*"*Create The Perfect Day *was such an incredible eye opening book. As a mom I was able to realize the power in planning and being able to achieve more than I realized I was capable of.*

Everyone needs this in their life!

~ Danielle Brockman

"Create the Perfect Day is a breath of fresh air! Using the planner made the difference for me. I recommend this to anyone who wants to see actual changes in a short period of time!"

~ Kayla Larsen

"In a world full of theory and conjecture, Create The Perfect Day is the quintessential step-by-step, day-by-day guide to propagate the changes needed to create your perfect life. Chock full of practical advice, the size of the book should not be dismissed. This is an ideal handbook to happiness, success, and ultimately fulfillment."

~ Kevin Smits

"As someone that has always struggled with time management, I found Create The Perfect Day to be very helpful. The question and answer portion of the book made it fun and easy for me to focus on what really matters to me, and break it down into daily segments rather than just broad goals. The format of the planner is incredible. I highly recommend connecting with Jessica and picking up your copy of Create The Perfect Day."

~ Gordon Hudelson

www.ingramcontent.com/pod-product-compliance
Lightning Source LLC
Chambersburg PA
CBHW051342200326

41521CB00015B/2590